JEWISH PENICILLIN

Mother Wonderful's

Profusely Illustrated Guide to
the Proper Preparation of

Chicken Soup

MYRA CHANIN

101 Production.
San Francisco

D1266473

Published simultaneously in
the United States and Canada

Published by 101 Productions
834 Mission Street, San Francisco CA 94103
Distributed to the book trade
in the United States
by The Scribner Book Companies, New York

Library of Congress Catalog Number: 84-042925

ISBN 89286-243-2

10 9 8 7 6 5 4 3 2 1

JEWISH PENICILLIN

Mother Wonderful's

Profusely Illustrated Guide to
the Proper Preparation of

Chicken Soup

For My Mother, Sylvia Daskell, the *Real* Mother Wonderful

With special thanks to my favorite butcher:
Jules Cohen, proprietor of Philadelphia's
Whitaker Kosher Meat Market.

EARLY ONE MORNING . . .
when you know your daughter is having a busy day,
call your daughter and say you're catching cold.
Ask if she can spare a few minutes
to drive you to a kosher butcher
so you can buy a chicken with feet for soup.

Everybody knows chicken soup
is the best defense against germs.

Wait outside in the cold
for your daughter.
When she drives up,
lean on your cane and . . .

Cough into your handkerchief.
Remember, you don't want to spread germs,
just guilt.

When you arrive at the butcher shop,
greet the owner as if he were your brother
rather than a person who intends
4   to sell you an inferior chicken.

Pretend to consider the chickens the butcher displays.
Pay no mind to claims of quality and freshness.

Everybody knows butchers hide their prime stock
"in the back" for their favorites.

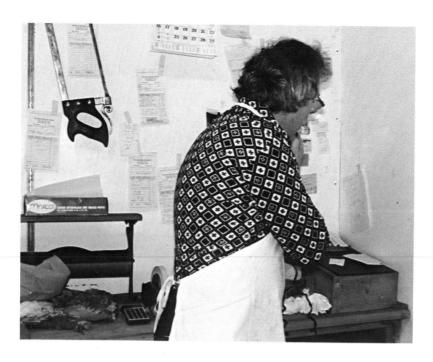

Bide your time. Concentrate.
Wait patiently until the telephone rings.
The butcher will be distracted and stop watching you.

While the butcher is talking on the phone
to another "wonderful" customer,
drop your cane and leap into the back.

Fling open the door to the walk-in box . . .

. . . and return victorious with your selection.

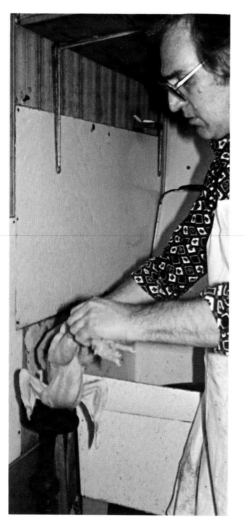

Follow the butcher
into the back and stare at him
while he singes the pin-feathers
off your bird.

He could switch your selection
with a regular chicken
should your eyes even blink.

Tell the butcher to include
a few extra feet
to give body to the soup.

If he says he has no extra feet,
tell him to cut them off
someone else's chicken.

Ask your daughter
if she can spare a few more minutes
so you can pick up a few fresh vegetables for your soup.

When she agrees, direct her to a market
on the other side of town.

Spend at least forty minutes
selecting two perfect carrots . . .

The right parsley root . . .

a fresh onion
and a small, crisp celery heart.

Let fourteen old folks step ahead of you
in the check-out line.

Tell your daughter that
a *mench* is never in such a hurry
that she doesn't have time to be a little considerate
of working people who have to buy food
for their families during lunch hour.

During the ride home, complain that
your kitchen is tiny
and all your pots are chipped.

Ask your daughter
if you could make soup at her house.
Ask her to stop at your building
so you can pick up a clean workdress.

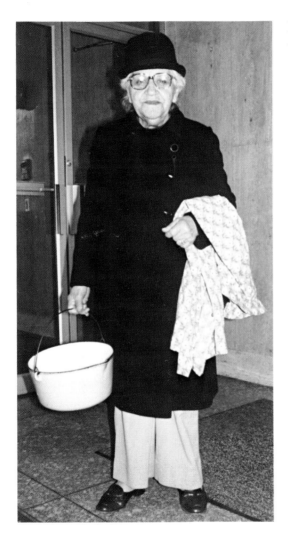

Return carrying
your favorite chipped pot.

Tell your daughter
you are going upstairs
to change your clothes.

Instead, make the beds.

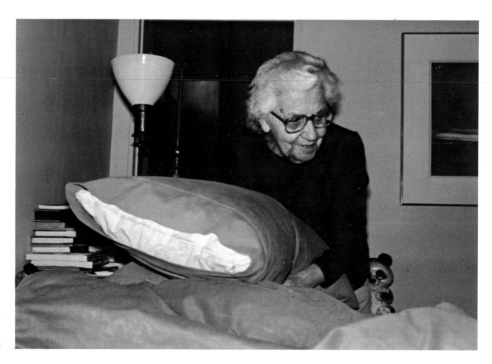

Pick up all books and magazines
laying open in the bedrooms.
Stack them in a neat pile with the titles facing the wall
so your daughter's family can't find
what they were reading.

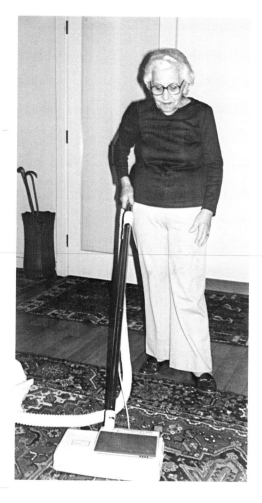

Vacuum the rugs
while your daughter attempts
to talk on the telephone.

Interrupt her conversation
to show her
how nice the house looks.
Tell her it only takes
a few minutes a day
to straighten up
and make everything shine.

When she screams at you,
innocently ask
how you offended her.

With tears in your eyes
limp into the kitchen.

Place the cut-up chicken in one bowl
Place the feet in another bowl.
They are dirtier.

Start to prepare the soup.

Pour some boiling water on the chicken parts.
Pour twice as much boiling water on the feet.

22 Rinse the boiling water off the chicken parts.

Scrape off the top layer of skin
with a sharp knife to remove
blemishes that eluded the butcher.

Rinse the feet three times.

With a different knife
peel the top layer of skin
from the feet.

Rinse the chicken parts again
because you touched them.
Transfer to a new, clean metal bowl.

Wash your hands
before and after you touch anything.

If you can't remember whether
you rinsed something off,
rinse it again to be safe.

Avoid adding germs to your soup.

Put the rinsed chicken parts in the bottom of
your rinsed chipped pot.
Rinse the feet one last time and place them on top.

Pour fresh boiling water into the pot.

Add vegetables and a little salt to the pot.
Rinse everything before adding but the salt
Worry whether the ingredients are clean.

Let the contents simmer,
lifting the lid every twenty-two seconds
to skim off anything that looks suspicious.

Check the progress of the soup
by placing your palm over the simmering liquid.
Burn the flesh of your inner arm
by letting it brush against the rim of the pot.

When no one is looking,
28 put on a pot of rice.

When you think the soup is ready, taste it.
Then make your grandson taste it.

Make your son-in-law taste it.

Make your daughter taste it.

After everyone agrees that
this is absolutely the best soup they have ever tasted,
wait forty-three seconds and ask
32 if they are *sure* the soup was all right.

Wrap up the beef Wellington your daughter
prepared for dinner and put it in the freezer.

Set out bowls and serve everyone soup.
When they ask why you aren't joining them, tell them
you'll eat after you finish cleaning the kitchen.

Stand over the table with a ladle
in your hand to refill bowls.

When you are not serving soup,
cut up the cooked chicken meat
and make chicken salad.

Your son-in-law loves
34 your chicken salad.

Pour one-half cup of the soup
into a tiny plastic container for yourself.

Place your chipped pot with the rest of the soup
in the front of your daughter's refrigerator,
near the chicken salad, so her family can find it
when they are hungry again.

Gather together your possessions
and the plastic container
with your half cup of soup.
Explain that you are
leaving the rest
in the ice-box for your grandson.
He really loves soup.

You understand that your daughter is too busy
with her important work to ever serve
the child anything but canned.

For you,
fresh chicken soup
is no big deal.
You can make it anytime.

Tsuni's Golden Chicken Soup

EQUIPMENT

1 8-quart kettle or soup pot with a tight-fitting lid, preferably rescued from the old country and brought in steerage to America

INGREDIENTS

Lots of boiling water for cleaning chicken

1 large kosher hen (5 to 6 pounds), with feet. If your butcher can't provide a stewing hen that large, add chicken parts to the one he gives you until you have 6 pounds of chicken.

6 to 8 extra chicken feet

2-1/2 quarts boiling water

1 large carrot (about 10 ounces), cut into 3 big chunks

1 large onion (about 10 ounces), peeled and left whole

3 crisp celery stalks, cut into 3-inch pieces

1 entire scallion, including greens

1 large parsley root with greens attached (about 4 ounces), peeled and cut in half lengthwise

About 1 ounce fresh dill, tied together for easy removal when soup is finished

1 tablespoon kosher salt

1/4 teaspoon white pepper

PREPARATION

Have your butcher cut the hen into 8 large pieces. Do not let him remove any fat from this chicken. You will remove excess fat later, but the soup has to cook with the fat for flavor.

Put the chicken feet in a bowl, cover them with boiling water and let them sit in the boiling water for at least 15 minutes. This will make them easier to peel. With a sharp knife, peel off the entire outer layer of tough yellow skin. Place the peeled feet in the bottom of your soup pot.

In another bowl, pour more boiling water over the chicken parts. Then scrape the skin with a small sharp knife to remove any pinfeathers still sticking to the skin and any dirt that adheres to the fatty skin from the processing of the chicken. Soaking and scraping the skin results in a much cleaner broth and almost no scum rising to the surface of the soup to be skimmed away during cooking.

COOKING

Add the cleaned chicken parts to the pot, including neck, neck skin, gizzard and liver. Add 2-1/2 quarts (10 cups) boiling water to the pot and cook uncovered over highest heat until the water comes to a boil again. Reduce heat slightly and let the chicken cook for about 5 minutes, skimming away any grey gook that rises to the surface. When the broth seems to be clear, add all other ingredients, cover the pot and reduce the heat so that the liquid simmers. Allow contents to simmer for 2-1/2 hours. It is not necessary to peek into the pot very often once you have adjusted the heat.

After 2-1/2 hours turn off heat. It doesn't hurt to let everything steep in the covered pot for another hour or so if you're not in a terrible rush. The soup will have tremendous body and flavor.

Remove the chicken and vegetables. Strain the soup back into the pot. If you want to remove most of the fat immediately from the top of the soup—you must leave a smidgen for color and flavor—pour the soup into a "souperstrainer," a plastic pitcher that pours from the bottom rather than the top. Otherwise, put the pot of soup in the refrigerator to cool until the fat congeals on top. Then just lift most of the fat off with a spatula.

Cook noodles or rice. Remove the chicken meat from the bones. If your family doesn't like boiled chicken added to the soup, make chicken salad from it. You can slice the cooked carrots and celery and add them to the soup when serving. When ready to serve, reheat the soup, taste and adjust seasoning with salt. Serve over noodles or rice, with cooked carrots, celery and chicken meat, if desired.

You will end up with about 8 cups of certified Jewish Penicillin which will serve 3 hungry ethnics— or 8 others.

Myra Chanin

Myra Chanin, Mother Wonderful, has been described as a cross between Julia Child and Woody Allen (or a Jewish Erma Bombeck). Author, humorist, award-winning baker, and television personality—the saga of her rise from obscurity is a tale of a midlife blossoming, which inspires everyone who hears it.

At 41, she was a depressed housewife whose marriage looked doomed. Her husband Alvin, that long-suffering saint, and Myra were not getting along. After ten years of marriage, she had raised her level of self-esteem and no longer agreed that Alvin was super-marvey and that she was a lucky woman to have the privilege of waiting on him.

She believed baking was the only skill she possessed to help her earn money and support herself in the event of a divorce. She went into the cheesecake business as Mother Wonderful, her cakes won awards and her marriage stabilized after Alvin realized that change would be less debilitating to him than losing half his assets.

Myra gave away her cheesecake business to attempt her heart's desire—writing humor. In 1980, her first book, *The Secret Life of Mother Wonderful* was published. In it she described her attempts to transform Alvin into Rhett Butler, a task only slightly less difficult than emptying the Atlantic Ocean into the Pacific Ocean with the aid of a sieve.

But cheesecake would not be denied and soon her second book, *Mother Wonderful's Cheesecakes and Other Goodies* appeared in bookstores and gourmet shops, and was greeted with cheers by food writers across the country.

The national promotional tours for both books turned her into a television personality, who now appears regularly with Gary Collins on Hour Magazine as well as on AM Philadelphia, Good Morning Los Angeles and The Morning Show in New York City. *Jewish Penicillin* grew out of an attempt to duplicate her mother's chicken soup for an appearance on Hour Magazine.